HEALTHY P COOKBOOK

THE TOP 50 MOST HEALTHY AND DELICIOUS PASTA RECIPES

By

ANITA HANSON

Copyright © 2015

Free Bonus

As a small symbol of thanks for buying this book,

I'd like to give a free bonus exclusive to my readers.

This Bonus is called **10 HEALTHY SMOOTHIE RECIPES**

What The Bonus Include?

- Recipe 1 - Mango Smoothie Surprise
- Recipe 2 - Blueberry Smoothie
- Recipe 3 - Peanut Butter and Banana
- Recipe 4 - Vanilla Yogurt and Blueberry
- Recipe 5 - Chocolate Raspberry
- Recipe 6 - Peach Smoothie
- Recipe 7 - Lemon-Orange Citrus
- Recipe 8 - Apple Smoothie
- Recipe 9 - Pineapple Smoothie
- Recipe 10 - Strawberry Smoothie

Download The Bonus From Here

http://www.elifemastery.com/10-healthy-smoothie-recipes/

Table of Contents

Time To Make Less Than 15 Minutes

Recipe 1 - Creamy Garlic Penne Pasta

Total Time: 15 Minutes

- **Preparation: 10 Mins**
- **Cooking: 5 Mins**

INGREDIENTS

1 (1 lb) box penne or 1 (1 lb) box penne rigate, cooked as directed, drained and kept hot

2 tbsps butter or 2 tbsps margarine

2 garlic cloves, minced

2 tbsps flour

3⁄4 cup chicken broth or 3⁄4 cup beef broth

3⁄4 cup milk

2 tsps parsley flakes

salt and pepper, to taste

1⁄3 cup grated parmesan cheese

DIRECTIONS

1. Melt butter and include garlic in a medium sauce pan.
2. Cook above medium for A single minute.
3. Include flour and cook A single minute, stirring frequently.
4. Stir in broth and milk and simmer, stirring regularly, right up until sauce boils and thickens.
5. Include parsley, salt, pepper and cheese.
6. Stir right up until cheese is melted.
7. Toss hot pasta with sauce and serve instantly.

Recipe 2 - Simple Pasta With Parmesan

Total Time: 15 Minutes

- **Preparation: 5 Mins**
- **Cooking: 10 Mins**

INGREDIENTS

1 lb pasta, cooked (any type)

3 -4 tbsps butter or 3 -4 tbsps olive oil

1⁄4-1⁄3 cup grated parmesan cheese

1⁄8-1⁄4 tsp garlic powder

fresh ground black pepper

DIRECTIONS

1. Place pasta into a microwavable dish big enough to provide you with a small room for stirring and tossing.
2. Dot pasta along with butter or drizzle along with olive oil.
3. Spread Parmesan over top. Include a lot of fresh-ground, black pepper.
4. Heat in microwave on high 3 to 5 minute each time, stirring regularly, right up until completely hot.
5. Serve, passing the pepper grinder at the kitchen table.

Recipe 3 - Fresh Tomato Pasta

Total Time: 15 Minutes

- **Preparation: 5 Mins**
- **Cooking: 10 Mins**

INGREDIENTS

2 -3 medium tomatoes

1 (8 ounce) package dry pasta

1 garlic clove

1 tsp dried basil

1 tbsp vegetable oil

DIRECTIONS

1. Put the garlic clove in a pan of salted water, bring the water to boil and include the rigatoni.
2. Cook right up until al dente.
3. Drain properly.
4. Return the pasta to the pan that the garlic was simmered inches.
5. While pasta is cooking, cut the tomato into pieces and put them in a little pan.
6. Spread the tomato chunks along with basil and put oil over the tomato.
7. Put tomatoes in the pan along with pasta.
8. Toss properly and eat while warm.

Recipe 4 - Bell Peppers and Pasta

Total Time: 15 Minutes

- **Preparation: 15 Mins**
- **Cooking: 0 Mins**

INGREDIENTS

2 1⁄4 cups raw penne pasta

3⁄4 cup chopped sweet onion

1 tbsp olive oil

3 garlic cloves, minced

1 cup chopped red bell pepper

1 cup chopped green pepper

1⁄4 cup sliced black olives

1 tsp dried oregano

1⁄4 tsp salt

1⁄8 tsp cayenne pepper

1⁄4 cup water

1⁄2 cup crumbled feta cheese

<u>DIRECTIONS</u>

1. Simmer and drain pasta.
2. In a non-stick skillet, sauté onion in oil for 1 1/2 minutes. Include garlic; cook Half a minute longer. Include red & green bell peppers; simmer & stir 3 minutes, right up until vegetables are tender.
3. Stir in olives, oregano, salt, and cayenne pepper.
4. Include water; cook and stir right up until mixture comes to a boil. Include drained pasta, take away from heat.
5. Stir in cheese; serve instantly.

Recipe 5 - Shrimp and Basil Pasta

Total Time: 15 Minutes

- **Preparation: 0 Mins**
- **Cooking: 15 Mins**

INGREDIENTS

8 ounces uncooked spaghetti or 8 ounces linguine

3⁄4 lb peeled and deveined shrimp

1⁄4 cup chopped fresh basil

3 tbsps drained capers

2 tbsps extra virgin olive oil

2 tbsps fresh lemon juice

1⁄2 tsp salt

Baby Spinach

DIRECTIONS

1. Bring 3 quarts water to a boil in a pot. Include pasta; simmer 8 minutes.
2. Include shrimp to pan; simmer 3 minutes or right up until shrimp are done and pasta is al dente. Drain.
3. Put pasta blend in a big pan.
4. Stir in basil and next 4 ingredients (through salt).
5. Put spinach on plates; top with pasta blend.

Recipe 6 - Fresh Tomatoes Pasta and Pine Nuts

Total Time: 15 Minutes

- **Preparation: 5 Mins**
- **Cooking: 10 Mins**

INGREDIENTS

2 medium tomatoes, diced

1 garlic clove, minced

2 tbsps olive oil

8 ounces angel hair pasta

2 tbsps pine nuts, toasted

coarse sea salt

fresh ground black pepper

DIRECTIONS

1. Bring a big pan of salted water to a boil.
2. At the same time, combine tomatoes, garlic and oil in a medium pan. Season with pepper and salt. Let stand a minimum of 10 minutes.
3. Simmer pasta in boiling water right up until al dente. Drain and return to pan. Include tomato blend and toss to mix.
4. Serve spread with pine nuts.

Recipe 7 – Pasta With Creamy White Cheese Sauce

Total Time: 7 Minutes

- **Preparation: 2 Mins**
- **Cooking: 5 Mins**

INGREDIENTS

1/2-2/3 cup whole wheat pasta

3 tbsps skim milk

1 tbsp nonfat sour cream

1 tsp whole wheat flour

2 tbsps grated low-fat cheese

salt

pepper

Suggested Additives

1 dash nutmeg

chicken

garlic

DIRECTIONS

1. Boil water after that include noddles in, cooking right up until preferred softness.
2. At the same time, put all the sauce ingredients into a sauce pot, heating at medium heat.
3. Blend right up until all ingredients are incorporated prior to allowing to cook and thicken, stirring frequently right up until at preferred thickness and cheese is melted and incorporated. Include more milk to cook if you want a thinner sauce. Include more cheese to taste if you desire.
4. Drain pasta and put sauce on pasta.

Recipe 8 - Sesame Pasta

Total Time: 15 Minutes

- **Preparation: 10 Mins**
- **Cooking: 5 Mins**

INGREDIENTS

1 tbsp sesame oil

8 ounces dry fettuccine pasta

1/2 tsp soy sauce

2 green onions, chopped

3/4 cup fresh bean sprouts

1 pinch cayenne pepper

1 pinch ground white pepper

1 pinch garlic powder

1 tbsp toasted sesame seeds

DIRECTIONS

1. Break fettucine noodles in two and put them in a big pan of boiling salted water.
2. Simmer right up until al dente, drain and wash.
3. Heat oil in frying pan or wok above medium heat. Include the soy sauce, green onions, bean sprouts, cayenne, pepper, garlic powder and pasta.
4. Stir and simmer for 2 to 3 minutes. Move to serving dishes and garnish along with toasted sesame seeds.

Time To Make Less Than 30 Minutes

Recipe 9 - Pasta and Peas

Total Time: 30 Minutes

- **Preparation: 15 Mins**
- **Cooking: 15 Mins**

INGREDIENTS

1 (16 ounce) package gemelli pasta

1/4 cup olive oil

3 green onions, chopped

1 pinch seasoned salt to taste (optional)

1 (15 ounce) can sweet peas, with liquid

1 bunch fresh basil, chopped

DIRECTIONS

1. Bring a big pan of lightly salted water to a boil. Include pasta and simmer for 8 to 10 mins or right up until al dente; drain.

2. Heat the olive oil in a saucepot above medium heat.

3. Stir in the green onions, as well as season along with seasoned salt. Simmer right up until green onions are golden brown.

4. Blend in the peas along with liquid and basil, as well as keep on simmering right up until heated through. Toss along with simmered pasta to serve.

Recipe 10 - Spicy Pasta

Total Time: 30 Minutes

- **Preparation: 10 Mins**
- **Cooking: 20 Mins**

INGREDIENTS

1 (12 ounce) package rotini pasta

1 tbsp vegetable oil

1 clove garlic, crushed

1 tsp dried basil

1 tsp Italian seasoning

1 onion, diced

2 red chile peppers, seeded and chopped

1 (14.5 ounce) can diced tomatoes

3 drops hot pepper sauce

salt and ground black pepper to taste

DIRECTIONS

1. Bring a big pan of lightly salted water to a boil. Simmer pasta in boiling water for 8 to 10 mins, or right up until al dente; drain.

2. At the same time, heat oil in a saucepot above medium heat.

3. Saute garlic along with basil and Italian seasoning for 2 to 3 mins.

4. Stir in onion and chiles; simmer right up until onion is tender.

5. Stir in tomatoes and hot sauce; cook for 5 mins, or right up until heated through. Toss along with the simmered pasta, as well as season along with pepper and salt.

Recipe 11 - Sharktooth Pasta

Total Time: 24 Minutes

- **Preparation: 12 Mins**
- **Cooking: 12 Mins**

INGREDIENTS

8 ounces dry farfalle (bow tie) pasta

1 (10.75 ounce) can condensed cream of chicken soup

1/4 cup milk

2 tbsps shredded Cheddar cheese

DIRECTIONS

1. Bring a big pan of lightly salted water to a boil. Include pasta and simmer for 8 to 10 mins or right up until al dente; drain.

2. Return pasta to pan; stir in soup and milk. Simmer and stir above medium heat right up until heated through.

3. Include cheese; simmer and stir just right up until cheese is melted. Serve hot.

Recipe 12 - Pasta with Asparagus

Total Time: 25 Minutes

- **Preparation: 15 Mins**
- **Cooking: 10 Mins**

INGREDIENTS

1 1/2 pounds fresh asparagus, trimmed and cut into 1 inch pieces

1/4 cup chicken broth

1/2 pound fresh mushrooms, sliced

8 ounces angel hair pasta

1 tbsp olive oil

1/2 tsp crushed red pepper

1/2 cup grated Parmesan cheese

DIRECTIONS

1. Simmer pasta in accordance to package directions.
2. Heat the olive oil in a nonstick frying pan.
3. Saute asparagus in the pot above medium heat for around 3 mins.
4. Include mushroom and chicken broth chunks; simmer 3 mins more.
5. Drain pasta, as well as move to a serving dish.
6. Lightly toss pasta along with asparagus mix; spread along with Parmesan and crushed red pepper.

Recipe 13 - Creamy Swiss Chard Pasta

Total Time: 20 Minutes

- **Preparation: 15 Mins**
- **Cooking: 5 Mins**

INGREDIENTS

1 lb swiss chard

1 tbsp olive oil

2 garlic cloves, smashed

1⁄4 cup onion, chopped

2 large tomatoes, chopped

1⁄2 cup fat free sour cream or 1⁄2 cup plain yogurt

1⁄2 cup 2% low-fat milk

1⁄4 cup parmesan cheese

8 ounces fettuccine pasta, cooked according to package

salt and pepper

DIRECTIONS

1. Wash swiss chard, slice into small chunks.
2. Heat oil in big 2 quart saucepot above medium high heat, 1 to 2 mins.
3. Include swiss chard, garlic and onion; simmering 1 to 2 mins, stirring from time to time.
4. Include tomatoes, sour cream, milk, parmesan cheese, simmered fettuccine, pepper and salt to taste; stir properly.
5. Serve hot.

Recipe 14 - Broccoli and Garlic Pasta

Total Time: 30 Minutes

- **Preparation: 15 Mins**
- **Cooking: 15 Mins**

INGREDIENTS

1 cup chicken broth

1⁄2 tsp dried basil

2 garlic cloves, minced

3 cups broccoli florets

4 1⁄2 cups hot cooked penne

1 tbsp lemon juice

parmesan cheese

black pepper (to taste)

DIRECTIONS

1. In a big frying pan, mix broth, basil, pepper, garlic and broccoli. Bring to a boil.
2. Cover up and simmer over low heat for 3 mins or right up until broccoli is tender crisp.
3. Include hot simmered pasta and juice of lemons. Toss to coat. Serve along with cheese.

Recipe 15 - Caprese Pasta

Total Time: 30 Minutes

- **Preparation: 10 Mins**
- **Cooking: 20 Mins**

INGREDIENTS

8 ounces buffalo mozzarella, brie or 8 ounces light cream cheese, cubed

1⁄2 cup fresh basil, snipped into ribbons

8 tomatoes, chopped

8 garlic cloves, chopped

1 tbsp olive oil, plus more to taste, as desired

fresh ground black pepper, to taste

1 lb linguine

DIRECTIONS

1. In a medium pan, mix your selection of cubed cheese along with the basil, olive oil, garlic, tomatoes, as well as black pepper, as well as stir properly, with a fork.
2. Include a little more olive oil, as preferred, to stop mix from getting too dry.
3. Permit sauce to sit while you make linguine in accordance to package directions.
4. Instantly right after draining linguine, toss along with sauce and permit to sit for a second while the cheese melts a little from the heat of the pasta.
5. Stir, serve, as well as enjoy!

Recipe 16 - Tuna Pasta Primavera

Total Time: 20 Minutes

- **Preparation: 10 Mins**
- **Cooking: 10 Mins**

INGREDIENTS

8 ounces bow tie pasta, uncooked

1 lb asparagus, cut into 1 inch pieces

1 cup English pea, frozen

1⁄4 cup green onion, sliced

1⁄2 tsp salt

2 tsps olive oil

1 cup tomatoes, chopped and seeded

1⁄4 cup lemon juice

2 (6 ounce) cans tuna in water, drained and coarsely flaked

1⁄2 tsp fresh ground black pepper

DIRECTIONS

1. Simmer pasta in accordance to package directions; drain but reserve 3 tbps of the simmering water.
2. While pasta simmers, mix peas and asparagus in a steamer basket over boiling water; cover up and steam 3-4 mins or right up until asparagus is crisp-tender. Drain.
3. Mix steamed onions, vegetables, salt, as well as oil in a big pan.
4. Include pasta, pasta simmering water, tomato, as well as juice of lemons; toss properly.
5. Include tuna; toss.
6. Spread along with pepper and serve.

Recipe 17 - Egyptian Pasta Stroganoff

Total Time: 25 Minutes

- **Preparation: 10 Mins**
- **Cooking: 15 Mins**

INGREDIENTS

1 lb ground chuck

1 onion, chopped

1 garlic clove, minced

4 cups beef consomme

3 tbsps soy sauce

1 tsp Worcestershire sauce

1 (4 ounce) can sliced mushrooms, drained

1 cup dry egyptian pasta

1⁄4 cup sour cream (to taste)

garlic salt

ground pepper

DIRECTIONS

1. In a medium pan brown ground chuck and onion. Include minced garlic when nearly finished. Drain.
2. Include leftover ingredients. Bring to a boil.
3. Lower heat, cover up and cook right up until rice/pasta is finished.
4. 15 mins Is dependent on what type of rice/pasta you're by using. Take a look at package directions.
5. When finished stir in sour cream.

Recipe 18 - Artichoke Pasta

Total Time: 30 Minutes

- **Preparation: 15 Mins**
- **Cooking: 15 Mins**

INGREDIENTS

4 ounces marinated artichokes

1 garlic clove, peeled and crushed

1 tbsp fresh parsley, finely chopped

1 tbsp thyme, finely chopped (leaves only)

1 lb linguine, cooked

1/2 lemon, juice of

parmesan cheese, shavings

DIRECTIONS

1. Put the artichokes, along with their oil into a pot and mash them down along using a fork.
2. Include parsley, the garlic and thyme and heat through for a couple of mins and right after that put over the hot pasta.
3. Include the juice of lemons and toss completely.
4. Serve in pans topped along with shavings of parmesan cheese.

Recipe 19 - Cajun Bean and Pasta Stew

Total Time: 25 Minutes

- **Preparation: 10 Mins**
- **Cooking: 15 Mins**

INGREDIENTS

1 (16 ounce) can black beans, drained

1 (16 ounce) can red beans, drained

1 (14 ounce) can diced tomatoes with green chilies

3⁄4 cup small shell pasta, uncooked

1⁄4 cup onion, chopped

1 tsp dried basil leaves

1 tsp Worcestershire sauce

1 garlic clove, finely chopped

1 -14 ounce vegetable broth

1⁄4 cup bell pepper, chopped

1⁄4 cup celery (chopped)

1 tsp cajun seasoning

DIRECTIONS

1. Blend all ingredients in a 2 quart saucepot.
2. Heat to boiling, stirring from time to time.
3. Lower heat.
4. Cover up and cook 15 mins, right up until macaroni is tender.

Recipe 20 - Jack-O-Lantern Pasta Dinner

Total Time: 30 Minutes

- **Preparation: 20 Mins**
- **Cooking: 10 Mins**

INGREDIENTS

6 -8 medium orange bell peppers, washed and dried

8 ounces orzo pasta or 8 ounces spaghetti

1 (25 ounce) jar pasta sauce, warmed (I love Mezzetta Napa Valley Bistro Tomato and Basil sauce)

DIRECTIONS

1. Carve each bell pepper as you would a Jack-O-Lantern, Shopping the top off and hollowing out the inside prior to carving a face.
2. Throw away the tops.
3. Simmer pasta in accordance to package directions.
4. Drain Pasta.
5. Blend pasta along with hot sauce and spoon into every individual pepper, ensuring the pasta 'oozes' out the eyes, mouth, as well as top of pepper.
6. Serve along with breadstick 'bones'--tie a knot by the end of each breadstick, bake, as well as enjoy!

Recipe 21 - Shrimp and Angel Hair Pasta

Total Time: 25 Minutes

- **Preparation: 5 Mins**
- **Cooking: 20 Mins**

INGREDIENTS

1 lb shrimp, peeled and deveined

1⁄2 cup white wine

1 tbsp crushed red pepper flakes (I used about 1/2 tblsp.)

2 tsps garlic, minced

3 tbsps olive oil

8 ounces angel hair pasta

4 green onions, diced

DIRECTIONS

1. Boil pasta to al dente.
2. In a non-stick frying pan mix shrimp, oil, pepper and garlic.
3. Simmer right up until shrimp is pink. .
4. During the last 2 mins of simmering include the wine and let the alcohol simmer out.
5. Toss the shrimp mix along with the pasta, top along with green onions and serve.

Recipe 22 - Pasta With Tasty Broccoli Sauce

Total Time: 20 Minutes

- **Preparation: 5 Mins**
- **Cooking: 15 Mins**

INGREDIENTS

2 tbsps olive oil

1 small onion, chopped

3 garlic cloves, minced

3⁄4 cup chicken broth (I use Oxo)

1 bunch broccoli, chopped

salt and pepper

1 tbsp lemon juice

1⁄4 cup parmesan cheese, grated

200 g pasta (I like whole wheat fettucini or spaghettini)

DIRECTIONS

1. In a medium saucepot simmer garlic and onion in olive oil over a low heat right up until onions are soft.
2. Include broccoli and chicken broth and bring to a boil, season along with pepper and salt.
3. Cover up and boil lightly for around 10 mins, or right up until broccoli is very tender, stir from time to time.
4. Put broccoli mix in a food processor or mixer along with juice of lemons and parmesan cheese. Pulse several times right up until smooth.
5. Toss pasta and sauce with each other and serve.
6. Enjoy!

Recipe 23 – Zucchini Pasta

Total Time: 17 Minutes

- **Preparation: 5 Mins**
- **Cooking: 12 Mins**

INGREDIENTS

16 ounces linguine

1 large zucchini

1 carrot

1 tbsp garlic, chopped

1⁄4 cup olive oil

parmesan cheese (lots)

salt and pepper

1 dash red pepper flakes

DIRECTIONS

1. Boil pasta in salted water.
2. While the pasta is simmering, make long carrot strips by using a vegetable peeler and shred the zucchini along with a cheese grater.
3. Drain the pasta.
4. By using the pasta pan, heat the olive oil, right after that include garlic, vegetables, red pepper flakes, pepper and salt.
5. Include pasta and toss, if you require more oil, include it right now.
6. Toss along with a entire bunch of parmesan cheese .
7. You could include prosciutto, chicken, mushrooms, shrimp, peas, broccoli.

Recipe 24 - Pasta with Scallops, Zucchini, and Tomatoes

Total Time: 30 Minutes

- **Preparation: 15 Mins**
- **Cooking: 15 Mins**

INGREDIENTS

1 pound dry fettuccine pasta

1/4 cup olive oil

3 cloves garlic, minced

2 zucchinis, diced

1/2 tsp salt

1/2 tsp crushed red pepper flakes

1 cup chopped fresh basil

4 roma (plum) tomatoes, chopped

1 pound bay scallops

2 tbsps grated Parmesan cheese

DIRECTIONS

1. In a big pan along with boiling salted water simmer pasta right up until al dente. Drain.

2. At the same time, in a big frying pan heat oil, include garlic and simmer right up until tender. Include the salt, red pepper flakes, zucchini, dried basil and saute for 10 mins. Include bay scallops, sliced tomatoes as well as fresh basil and cook for 5 mins, or right up until scallops are opaque.

3. Put sauce over simmered pasta and serve along with grated Parmesan cheese.

Recipe 25 - Bucatini Pasta with Shrimp and Anchovies

Total Time: 25 Minutes

- **Preparation: 10 Mins**
- **Cooking: 15 Mins**

INGREDIENTS

1 pound bucatini pasta

1 (2 ounce) can anchovy fillets, oil reserved

1 tsp red pepper flakes, or to taste

3 cloves garlic, minced

2 zucchini, halved lengthwise and cut in 1/4 inch slices

1 pint grape tomatoes

2 tsps dried oregano

2 tsps dried basil

1 pound peeled and deveined medium shrimp

DIRECTIONS

1. Bring a big pan of lightly salted water to a boil. Include pasta and simmer for 8 to 10 mins or right up until al dente; drain.

2. At the same time, stir with each other the anchovies and their oil along with the red pepper flakes and garlic in a big frying pan above medium heat, breaking up the anchovies as you stir.

3. Once the garlic begins to sizzle, include the cut zucchini, as well as simmer right up until it begins to soften, around 3 mins.

4. Stir in the grape tomatoes, as well as keep on simmering right up until the zucchini is tender, as well as the skins of the tomatoes begin to pop, 5 mins more.

5. Spread the vegetable mix along with oregano and basil, right after that stir in shrimp. Simmer right up until the shrimp turn pink and are no longer translucent.

6. Put over bucatini to serve.

Recipe 26 - Roasted Veggie Pasta

Total Time: 30 Minutes

- **Preparation: 15 Mins**
- **Cooking: 15 Mins**

INGREDIENTS

1/4 pound fresh asparagus

2 red bell pepper, sliced

1/4 pound crimini mushrooms, sliced

10 cloves roasted garlic, chopped

1/2 tomato, quartered

1/2 tsp chopped fresh rosemary

1/2 tsp chopped fresh oregano

2 tbsps olive oil

8 ounces dry fettuccini noodles

1/4 cup grated Parmesan cheese

2 tbsps tapenade

DIRECTIONS

1. Preheat stove to 350 degrees Fahrenheit. Make asparagus by cutting off woody base and chopping diagonally into 4 inch chunks.

2. In a roasting pot, mix bell pepper, asparagus, roasted garlic, mushrooms, and tomato. Spread along with oregano and rosemary, right after that drizzle along with olive oil. Bake in preheated stove for 15 mins.

3. Bring a big pan of lightly salted water to a boil. Include pasta and simmer for 8 to 10 mins or right up until al dente; drain. Toss along with tapenade, Parmesan cheese and roasted vegetables.

Recipe 27 - Pasta with Fresh Tomato Sauce

Total Time: 25 Minutes

- **Preparation: 15 Mins**
- **Cooking: 10 Mins**

INGREDIENTS

1 (16 ounce) package dry penne pasta

8 roma (plum) tomatoes, diced

1/2 cup Italian dressing

1/4 cup finely chopped fresh basil

1/4 cup diced red onion

1/4 cup grated Parmesan cheese

DIRECTIONS

1. Bring a big pan of lightly salted water to a boil. Put the penne pasta in the pan, simmer 10 mins, right up until al dente, as well as drain.
2. In a big pan, toss the simmered pasta along with the tomatoes, Italian dressing, basil, red onion, as well as Parmesan cheese.

Recipe 28 - Cajun Pasta Fresca

Total Time: 25 Minutes

- **Preparation: 5 Mins**
- **Cooking: 20 Mins**

INGREDIENTS

1 pound vermicelli pasta

2 tbsps olive oil

1 tsp minced garlic

13 roma (plum) tomatoes, chopped

1 tbsp salt

1 tbsp chopped fresh parsley

1 tbsp Cajun seasoning

1/2 cup shredded mozzarella cheese

1/2 cup grated Parmesan cheese

DIRECTIONS

1. Bring a big pan of lightly salted water to a boil. Include pasta and simmer for 8 to 10 mins or right up until al dente; drain.

2. While the pasta water is boiling, in a big frying pan above medium heat, briefly saute garlic in oil. Stir in tomatoes and their juice and spread along with salt. When tomatoes are bubbly, mash slightly using a fork. Stir in parsley, lower heat and cook 5 mins more.

3. Toss hot pasta along with tomato sauce, Cajun seasoning, mozzarella and Parmesan.

Recipe 29 - Pesto Pasta with Chicken

Total Time: 30 Minutes

- **Preparation: 10 Mins**
- **Cooking: 20 Mins**

INGREDIENTS

1 (16 ounce) package bow tie pasta

1 tsp olive oil

2 cloves garlic, minced

2 boneless skinless chicken breasts, cut into bite-size pieces

crushed red pepper flakes to taste

1/3 cup oil-packed sun-dried tomatoes, drained and cut into strips

1/2 cup pesto sauce

DIRECTIONS

1. Bring a big pan of lightly salted water to a boil. Include pasta and simmer for 8 to 10 mins or right up until al dente; drain.

2. Heat oil in a big frying pan above medium heat. Saute garlic right up until tender, right after that stir in chicken. Season along with red pepper flakes. Simmer right up until chicken is golden, as well as simmered through.

3. In a big pan, mix pasta, sun-dried tomatoes, chicken, and pesto. Toss to coat equally.

Recipe 30 - Southwestern Vegetarian Pasta

Total Time: 20 Minutes

- **Preparation: 10 Mins**
- **Cooking: 20 Mins**

INGREDIENTS

1 tbsp vegetable oil

1 onion, chopped

1/2 green bell pepper, diced

2 cloves garlic, chopped

2 tbsps chili powder

1 tsp ground cumin

1 (28 ounce) can diced tomatoes with juice

1 (15 ounce) can chickpeas

1 (10 ounce) package frozen corn kernels, thawed

1 (12 ounce) package uncooked elbow macaroni

1/2 cup shredded Monterey Jack cheese

DIRECTIONS

1. Heat oil in a big, deep frying pan. Saute green pepper, onion, chili powder, garlic and cumin. Stir in chickpeas, tomatoes and corn. Lower heat to low and cook 15 to 20 mins, or right up until thickened and heated through.

2. At the same time, bring a big pan of lightly salted water to a boil. Include macaroni and simmer for 8 to 10 mins or right up until al dente; drain.

3. Mix pasta and sauce. Spread each serving along with Monterey Jack cheese.

Recipe 31 - Creamy Smoked Salmon Pasta

Total Time: 30 Minutes

- **Preparation: 15 Mins**
- **Cooking: 15 Mins**

INGREDIENTS

6 tbsps butter

1/2 onion, finely chopped

2 tbsps all-purpose flour

2 tsps garlic powder

2 cups skim milk

1/2 cup grated Romano cheese

1 cup frozen green peas, thawed and drained

1/2 cup canned mushrooms, drained

10 ounces smoked salmon, chopped

1 (16 ounce) package penne pasta

DIRECTIONS

1. Bring a big pan of lightly salted water to a boil. Include pasta and simmer for 8 to 10 mins or right up until al dente; drain.
2. Melt butter in a big frying pan above medium heat. Saute onion in butter right up until tender.
3. Stir garlic powder and flour into the onions and butter. Slowly stir in milk. Heat to just underneath boiling stage, as well as right after that slowly stir in cheese right up until the sauce is smooth. Stir in mushrooms and peas. As well as simmer over low heat for 4 mins.
4. Toss in smoked salmon, as well as simmer for 2 more mins. Serve over pasta.

Recipe 32 - Herb and Chicken Pasta

Total Time: 30 Minutes

- **Preparation: 15 Mins**
- **Cooking: 15 Mins**

INGREDIENTS

1 (16 ounce) package angel hair pasta

4 skinless, boneless chicken breast halves

salt and pepper to taste

1/2 tsp dried basil

1/2 tsp dried rosemary

1/2 tsp Cajun seasoning (optional)

1/2 tsp crushed red pepper flakes (optional)

1/4 cup olive oil

3 cloves garlic, chopped

1 onion, chopped

1 cup chicken broth

DIRECTIONS

1. Bring a big pan of lightly salted water to a boil. Include pasta and simmer for 8 to 10 mins or right up until al dente; drain and reserve.

2. At the same time, season chicken along with rosemary, basil, pepper and salt and, Cajun seasoning, as well as red pepper flakes. Heat oil in a big frying pan above medium heat; include chicken and simmer right up until browned. Take away chicken from frying pan and stir in onions and garlic; simmer and stir right up until clear.

3. Return chicken to frying pan over onion mix and include broth. Cook right up until chicken is simmered through and no more pink inside; sprinkle mix on pasta and serve.

Recipe 33 - Penne Pasta with Spinach and Bacon

Total Time: 25 Minutes

- **Preparation: 10 Mins**
- **Cooking: 15 Mins**

INGREDIENTS

1 (12 ounce) package penne pasta

2 tbsps olive oil, divided

6 slices bacon, chopped

2 tbsps minced garlic

1 (14.5 ounce) can diced tomatoes

1 bunch fresh spinach, rinsed and torn into bite-size pieces

DIRECTIONS

1. Bring a big pan of lightly salted water to a boil. Include the penne pasta, as well as simmer right up until tender, 8 to 10 mins.

2. At the same time, heat 1 tbp of olive oil in a frying pan above medium heat. Put bacon in the frying pan, as well as simmer right up until browned and crisp. Include garlic, as well as simmer for around a single minute. Stir in the tomatoes, as well as simmer right up until heated through.

3. Put the spinach into a colander, as well as drain the hot pasta over it so it is wilted. Move to a big serving pan, as well as toss with the leftover olive oil, as well as the bacon and tomato mix.

Recipe 34 - Fire Roasted Tomato and Feta Pasta with Shrimp

Total Time: 27 Minutes

- **Preparation: 15 Mins**
- **Cooking: 12 Mins**

INGREDIENTS

1/2 pound linguine pasta

1 tbsp olive oil

3 cloves garlic, minced

12 medium shrimp, peeled and deveined

1 (14.5 ounce) can fire roasted tomatoes

1 tbsp chopped fresh basil

salt and pepper to taste

1/2 cup crumbled feta cheese

DIRECTIONS

1. Bring a big pan of lightly salted water to a boil. Include pasta and simmer for 8 to 10 mins or right up until al dente; drain.

2. While the pasta is simmering, heat the olive oil in a big frying pan above medium heat. Include the garlic; simmer and stir right up until fragrant, around a single minute. Include the shrimp, as well as simmer right up until opaque, around 3 to 5 mins. Put in the tomatoes and heat through. Season with basil, pepper and salt.

3. Toss the simmered pasta in the sauce, as well as spread with crumbled feta to serve.

Recipe 35 – Greek Chicken Pasta

Total Time: 30 Minutes

- **Preparation: 15 Mins**
- **Cooking: 15 Mins**

INGREDIENTS

1 (16 ounce) package linguine pasta

1/2 cup chopped red onion

1 tbsp olive oil

2 cloves garlic, crushed

1 pound skinless, boneless chicken breast meat - cut into bite-size pieces

1 (14 ounce) can marinated artichoke hearts, drained and chopped

1 large tomato, chopped

1/2 cup crumbled feta cheese

3 tbsps chopped fresh parsley

2 tbsps lemon juice

2 tsps dried oregano

salt and pepper to taste

2 lemons, wedged, for garnish

<u>*DIRECTIONS*</u>

1. Bring a big pan of lightly salted water to a boil. Simmer pasta in boiling water right up until tender yet firm to the bit, 8 to 10 mins; drain.

2. Heat olive oil in a big frying pan above medium-high heat. Include onion and garlic; saute right up until fragrant, around 2 mins. Stir in the chicken and simmer, stirring from time to time, right up until chicken is no more pink in the center and the juices run clear, around 5 to 6 mins.

3. Lower heat to medium-low; include artichoke hearts, tomato, feta cheese, parsley, juice of lemons, oregano, as well as simmered pasta. Simmer and stir right up until heated through, around 2 to 3 mins. Take away from heat, season with pepper and salt, as well as garnish with lemon wedges.

Time To Make Less Than 60 Minutes

Recipe 36 - Souper Skillet Pasta

Total Time: 35 Minutes

- **Preparation: 15 Mins**
- **Cooking: 20 Mins**

INGREDIENTS

1 envelope Lipton Onion Soup Mix

1 lb ground beef

1 tsp oregano

1 (28 ounce) can tomatoes, undrained (I use the diced ones)

2 cups water

1 1/2 cups elbow macaroni

1/3 cup grated parmesan cheese

mozzarella cheese

DIRECTIONS

1. In big frypot, brown ground beef;drain;include onion soup blend ,oregano, tomatoes and water.
2. Bring to a boil, stir in macaroni.
3. Cook cover up, stirring from time to time for 20 mins or right up until macaroni is tender.
4. Stir in parmesan cheese and top with grated mozzarella.

Recipe 37 - Pasta Amatriciana

Total Time: 45 Minutes

- **Preparation: 15 Mins**
- **Cooking: 30 Mins**

INGREDIENTS

2 tbsps olive oil

1 medium onion, chopped

3 garlic cloves, chopped (you can vary the amount depending on how much you like garlic)

4 slices bacon, chopped (do not use maple-flavored bacon)

3⁄4 cup white wine

1 (28 ounce) can tomato puree

red pepper flakes

DIRECTIONS

1. Put enough olive oil in a big sauce pot to cover up the bottom and heat above medium flame.
2. Put onions, garlic and bacon in pot and saute for around 5 mins or right up until bacon is simmered through.
3. Include wine and bring to a boil for around 3-4 mins.
4. Include tomatoes and right after that fill the empty tomato can around halfway with water and include to pot.
5. Include as much or as little red pepper flakes as you like.
6. Cook over low heat for around 1/2 hour.
7. Serve with penne pasta (or pasta of your selection).

Recipe 38 - Pasta With Eggplant

Total Time: 50 Minutes

- **Preparation: 10 Mins**
- **Cooking: 40 Mins**

INGREDIENTS

4 tbsps olive oil

1 large eggplant, peeled and cut into 3/4 inch cubes

1 lb ziti pasta

4 garlic cloves, peeled and chopped

1 onion, peeled and diced

1 (28 ounce) can tomatoes with juice

12 kalamata olives, pitted and chopped

salt & freshly ground black pepper

1/4 cup chopped fresh basil

DIRECTIONS

1. Heat 3 tbps of the olive oil in a big, deep frying pan.
2. Include the eggplant cubes and simmer, stirring, right up until golden brown, around 15 to 18 mins.
3. At the same time, simmer the ziti in accordance to package directions.
4. Whenever it is al dente, drain.
5. Take away the eggplant from the saute pot.
6. Include the onion and the garlic, along with the leftover 1 tbp of olive oil, as well as simmer for 3 mins, stirring.
7. Include the tomatoes and smash them using your fingers.
8. Include the simmered the olives and eggplant cubes.
9. Simmer and stir 15 mins, right up until sauce is thick.
10. Season with pepper and salt.
11. Stir in the basil.
12. Simmer 2 mins.
13. Include the ziti to the sauce and stir to mix.
14. Serve hot.

Recipe 39 - Spicy Crab over Pasta

Total Time: 40 Minutes

- **Preparation: 20 Mins**
- **Cooking: 20 Mins**

INGREDIENTS

1 tbsp olive oil

2 medium garlic cloves, pressed

1/2 medium green bell pepper, diced very small

1 tsp crushed red pepper flakes (I add a little more)

1 (16 ounce) can whole tomatoes

1/2 cup salt-free fish stock

1 tbsp tomato paste

1 tbsp fresh parsley, finely chopped

2 tsps sugar

1 tsp finely grated lemon zest

1 bay leaf

1/2 lb flaked crabmeat, with bones removed

cooked pasta, of your choice

DIRECTIONS

1. In a big frying pan or saucepot, heat the oil with bell pepper, red pepper flakes and the garlic over moderate heat.
2. Whenever they sizzle, include the tomatoes, smashing them using your hands.
3. Stir in tomato paste, the fish stock, sugar, parsley, bay leaf and lemon zest.
4. Cook for 7 to 10 mins, right up until thick but still pretty liquid.
5. Right after that stir in the crabmeat and keep on cooking right up until the sauce is thick, 3-5 mins more.
6. Serve over hot simmered pasta for example linguine, fettuccine, spaghetti, or fettuccelli.

Recipe 40 - Italian Pasta Stir-Fry

Total Time: 60 Minutes

- **Preparation: 30 Mins**
- **Cooking: 30 Mins**

INGREDIENTS

8 ounces linguine, uncooked

2 medium tomatoes, seeded and chopped

1 medium onion, chopped

1 medium zucchini, sliced

1/4 cup snipped fresh parsley

1 tbsp olive oil

2 cloves garlic, pressed

1 tsp dried basil

1 tsp oregano leaves

1/8 tsp salt

1/8 tsp ground black pepper

1/4 cup grated fresh parmesan cheese

DIRECTIONS

1. Simmer linguine in accordance to package directions.
2. Drain and keep hot.
3. Chop tomatoes and onion.
4. Cut zucchini.
5. Snip parsley.
6. Heat oil in a stir-fry frying pan above medium heat right up until hot.
7. Include pressed garlic to frying pan; stir-fry for 15 seconds.
8. Include zucchini and onion; stir-fry 2-3 mins or right up until vegetables are crisp-tender.
9. Include tomatoes, parsley and seasonings.
10. Heat 1-2 mins, stirring lightly right up until heated through.
11. Take away from heat.
12. Stir in linguine.
13. Grate parmesan cheese over pasta.
14. Serve instantly.

Recipe 41 - Semolina Pasta

Total Time: 32 Minutes

- **Preparation: 30 Mins**
- **Cooking: 2 Mins**

INGREDIENTS

3 eggs

1⁄8 tsp salt

1 3⁄4 cups semolina flour

DIRECTIONS

1. Beat the eggs in a medium size pan using a fork.
2. Blend in the salt.
3. Include the pasta flour a little each time, blending properly.
4. Knead the dough 5 mins.
5. Wrap in wax paper and let it rest for 12 mins.
6. Right after that pass through your dough through a pasta machine or lightly roll dough out as thin as you could on a floured surface with a rolling pin.
7. Slice into size of noodles required.
8. If making Ravioli brush edges with egg white to seal.
9. Amount given for ravioli.

Recipe 42 – Pasta with mushrooms and spinach

Total Time: 33 Minutes

- **Preparation: 15 Mins**
- **Cooking: 18 Mins**

INGREDIENTS

8 ounces pasta, i use farfalle or penne

2 tbsps olive oil

8 ounces mixed mushrooms, eg,oyster,shitake and field,thickly sliced

2 cloves crushed garlic

4 ounces baby spinach leaves, washed and dried

6 sun-dried tomatoes, finely chopped (in oil)

salt

freshly ground black pepper

fresh basil leaf (for garnish)

halved cherry tomatoes (for garnish)

DIRECTIONS

1. Simmer the pasta in lightly salted boiling water according to packet directions.
2. At the same time, heat the oil in a big frying pot, rapidly fry the garlic and mushrooms over a high heat for 2-3 mins, right up until just simmered.
3. Include the spinach and stir right up until simply wilted, stir in the sun dried out tomatoes and season to taste.
4. Drain out pasta and toss into the spinach and mushroom mix.
5. End up as a serving plate, as well as garnish with the halved cherry tomatoes and torn basil leaves.

Recipe 43 - Grilled Chicken Penne Pasta

Total Time: 45 Minutes

- **Preparation: 20 Mins**
- **Cooking: 25 Mins**

INGREDIENTS

1/2 medium yellow onion, finely chopped

4 garlic cloves, minced

1 (14 1/2 ounce) can tomatoes, diced

1 (14 1/2 ounce) can tomato sauce

1 (6 ounce) can tomato juice

2 tbsps basil, chopped fresh

1 tbsp olive oil

1 tbsp parsley, chopped fresh

fresh ground black pepper, to-taste

1 tsp salt

2 chicken breasts, grilled and sliced

2 cups penne pasta

parmesan cheese, grated

DIRECTIONS

1. Sauté onions in olive oil right up until translucent.
2. Include garlic and simmer for one more minute.
3. Include tomato, tomato juice, black pepper, tomato sauce, basil, salt, as well as parsley.
4. Once sauce boils lower to cook and include grilled chicken.
5. Cook right up until pasta is simmered.
6. Simmer penne pasta in salted boiling water.
7. Strain pasta and include to sauce.
8. Serve garnished with Parmesan cheese.

Recipe 44 - Lemon Shrimp With Pasta and Basil

Total Time: 40 Minutes

- **Preparation: 20 Mins**
- **Cooking: 20 Mins**

INGREDIENTS

1 medium cooking onion, chopped and sauteed

2 cups bulgur (add 4 cups of boiled water in a bowl and set aside)

3 freshly squeezed lemons

1/2 cup finely chopped parsley

1 large tomatoes, diced

1/4 tsp cumin

1/4 tsp coriander

1/4 tsp paprika

1 cup quartered red seedless grapes or 1 cup quartered green seedless grape

1/4 cup extra virgin olive oil

salt

DIRECTIONS

1. Simmer pasta in a big pot of boiling water for 10 mins or right up until al dente.
2. Include shrimp and drain instantly.
3. Return pasta mix to the pot.
4. Mix next 5 ingredients in a pan.
5. Toss with simmered pasta and shrimp.
6. Spread cheese over pasta and serve instantly.

Recipe 45 - Broccoli and Pasta Bianco

Total Time: 55 Minutes

- **Preparation: 30 Mins**
- **Cooking: 25 Mins**

INGREDIENTS

1 lb penne pasta

1 (1 lb) bag frozen broccoli

1 (10 3/4 ounce) can cream of mushroom soup

1 1/2 cups nonfat milk

1/2 tsp black pepper

1 1/2 cups shredded mozzarella cheese

1/4 cup shredded parmesan cheese

DIRECTIONS

1. Simmer penne pasta in accordance to directions on package.
2. Include broccoli to simmering pasta for the last 5 mins or so of simmering time; drain.
3. Blend soup, milk and pepper in 2 quart shallow baking dish.
4. Include pasta/broccoli blend, 3/4 cup mozzarella cheese and 2 TBSP Parmesan cheese; blend lightly.
5. Top with leftover cheeses.
6. Preheat stove to 350°F.
7. Bake, uncover, for 25 mins, or right up until cheese is melted.

Recipe 46 - Zucchini, Mushroom, and Fresh Tomato Sauce over Pasta

Total Time: 50 Minutes

- **Preparation: 30 Mins**
- **Cooking: 20 Mins**

INGREDIENTS

2 tbsps olive oil

1/2 cup chopped onion

1 cup diced trimmed zucchini (1 1/2 inch dice)

1 cup diced mushroom

2 garlic cloves, minced

1 cup chopped fresh tomato

1/2 tsp salt

1/4 cup chopped fresh Italian parsley

2 tbsps chopped fresh basil

1 lb penne, cooked al dente and drained

grated parmesan cheese

DIRECTIONS

1. Heat the oil in a wide saucepot; include in onion; stir/saute 5 mins.
2. Stir in mushrooms and zucchini; saute over high heat, stirring, right up until tender, around 10 mins.
3. Stir in garlic; saute a single minute.
4. Include in tomatoes; simmer/stir 5 mins.
5. Include in salt, parsley, as well as basil.
6. Toss warm pasta with the sauce; serve instantly; spread grated parmesan on top.

Recipe 47 - Cajun Pasta

Total Time: 55 Minutes

- **Preparation: 20 Mins**
- **Cooking: 35 Mins**

INGREDIENTS

2 tbsps olive oil

3⁄4 lb boneless skinless chicken breast, cut into 1-inch pieces

1⁄2 lb hot Italian sausage, sliced

1⁄2 lb asparagus, cut into 1-inch pieces

1 medium onion, cut into 1-inch pieces

1 medium bell pepper, cored, seeded and cut into 1-inch pieces

1 small zucchini, cut into 1-inch pieces

29 ounces diced tomatoes with jalapenos

2 garlic cloves, peeled and chopped fine

1 tsp dried oregano

1⁄2 tsp paprika

1⁄2 tsp black pepper

1⁄2 lb linguine, cooked

parmesan cheese, grated, if desired (optional)

DIRECTIONS

1. Heat olive oil in a big frying pan. Include the chicken and sausage; simmer for around 5 mins turning once.
2. Include the asparagus, onion, bell pepper, zucchini, diced tomatoes, garlic, oregano, paprika and black pepper. Stir properly.
3. Bring to a boil. Lower heat to medium and cook for around 30 mins or right up until all the vegetables are tender. Stirring from time to time.
4. Toss with simmered linguine. Serve with cheese if preferred.

Recipe 48 - Pasta Genovese

Total Time: 35 Minutes

- **Preparation: 15 Mins**
- **Cooking: 20 Mins**

INGREDIENTS

2 ounces minced garlic

1 ounce olive oil

3 ounces sun-dried tomatoes (In Oil)

1 ounce pine nuts

10 ounces cleaned spinach leaves

2 lbs plum tomatoes, quartered, seeded

1 lb penne, cooked al dente

2 ounces romano cheese

1 ounce parmesan cheese

1/8 tsp black pepper

1/8 tsp salt

DIRECTIONS

1. Heat oil in a frying pan and simmer pine nuts right up until golden brown.
2. Include garlic and spinach and simmer right up until slightly wilted.
3. Include salt, pepper, plum tomatoes as well as sun-dried out tomatoes.
4. Bring this to a boil for around 5 mins.
5. Include pasta and stir right up until properly blended.
6. Simmer right up until heated and include cheeses.
7. Taste and adjust seasonings and serve hot.

Recipe 49 - Sesame Chicken and Asparagus Pasta

Total Time: 50 Minutes

- **Preparation: 20 Mins**
- **Cooking: 30 Mins**

INGREDIENTS

8 ounces linguine

3 garlic cloves, minced

1 tbsp red wine vinegar

1 tbsp brown sugar

6 tbsps chunky peanut butter

1⁄4 cup soy sauce

6 tbsps sesame oil

1 tbsp hot chili oil (optional)

2 cooked boneless skinless chicken breast halves

5 tbsps sesame seeds, toasted

1 lb thin asparagus, trimmed

3 scallions, white bulb and inches green cut up

1 small cucumber, halved and seeded cut into 1/4 inch dice

DIRECTIONS

1. Bring a big pan of water to boil. Include the linguine and simmer right up until just tender. Drain and wash under cold water. Drain again, as well as set aside in a big blending pan.

2. Put vinegar, the garlic, peanut butter, soy sauce and brown sugar in a food processor. Process for a minute. With motor working, gradually include the sesame and chile oils via the feed tube, as well as process right up until properly mixed.

3. Cut the chicken into two inc julienne and toss along with linguine. four T of the sesame seeds and Include the sauce and toss to coat properly.

4. Slice the asaragus on a diagonal into a single inch. Blanch in a saucepot of boiling water for 1 mins. Drain, wash beneath cold water as well as pat dry.

5. Put the chicken and linguine in a big flat serving pan and organize the asaragus on top. Spread with cucumber, scallions and leftover sesame seeds.

Recipe 50 - Baked Pasta & Cheese With Tomatoes

Total Time: 55 Minutes

- **Preparation: 15 Mins**
- **Cooking: 40 Mins**

INGREDIENTS

16 ounces pasta (pinwheel, cooked al dente)

28 ounces tomatoes (herbs & spices, pureed)

2 cups mozzarella cheese (grated)

1 large white onion (finely chopped)

1⁄4 cup Parmigiano-Reggiano cheese (grated)

1⁄4 cup half-and-half cream (or whole milk)

2 tbsps basil pesto

2 tbsps garlic (crushed)

salt

pepper

DIRECTIONS

1. Preheat stove at 375.
2. Butter a 9 x 13 casserole plate.
3. Simmer pinwheel pasta in salted wated right up until "al dente", reserve.
4. Finely chop the onion, reserve.
5. In food processor, puree the tomatoes right up until smooth.
6. In big pan, blend with each other the garlic, pureed tomatoes, basil pesto, onions and the simmered pasta. Include pepper and salt to taste.
7. Move to buttered casserole.
8. Grate parmesan cheese and mozzarella cheese.
9. Include cheeses on top of casserole.
10. Bake for 30 mins and enjoy.

The End and More

We reached the end of the book, I hope you enjoyed it.

Here are some authors, sources and books that helped me to write this book:

20 Healthy Copycat Restaurant Recipes: Healthy Homemade Copycat Recipes From Famous Restaurants, Bring Your Favorite Restaurant To Your Home Kindle Edition

by Maira Benjamin

Food.com

Slow Cooker Recipes: 30 Of The Most Healthy And Delicious Slow Cooker Recipes: Includes New Recipes For 2015 With Fantastic Ingredients Kindle Edition

by Stacey Turner

allrecipes.com

The Clean Eating Cookbook & Diet: Over 100 Healthy Whole Food Recipes & Meal Plans

recipe.com

The Skinnytaste Cookbook: Light on Calories, Big on Flavor Kindle Edition

by Gina Homolka

Clean Food Diet: Avoid processed foods and eat clean with few simple lifestyle changes(free nutrition recipes)(natural food recipes) (Special Diet Cookbooks & Vegetarian Recipes Collection Book 4) Kindle Edition

by Jonathan Vine

Conclusion

Thank you again for downloading the book.

Finally. I hope you enjoyed this book. **Please take the time to share your thoughts and post a review on Amazon. It'd be greatly appreciated.**

Thank you and good luck !

Anita.

Printed in Great Britain
by Amazon.co.uk, Ltd.,
Marston Gate.